Carole Reeve

CU00405641

St Augustine

Apostle to the English
597-1997

The Parish of St Augustine of Canterbury, Whitton

Cover illustration

St Augustine of Canterbury

From an icon painted by Brother Aidan

(Reproduced with kind permission of the artist)

Published by

The Parish of St Augustine of Canterbury, Whitton

Hospital Bridge Road, Whitton, Middlesex TW2 6DE

Copyright © Carole Reeves 1997

ISBN 0 9529898 0 8

First published 1997

Designed and typeset by

Reality Graphics Ltd

41 Chobham Road, Woking, Surrey GU21 1JD

Printed by

Optichrome Ltd

Maybury Road, Woking, Surrey GU21 5HX

Contents

Erratum ~ This page replaces page 5

Contents

Foreword

As the 103rd Archbishop of Canterbury may I congratulate Carole Reeves for all she has done in writing such a well researched and readable book. The story of England's first Archbishop deserves to be told and my hope is that this will be read far beyond the boundaries of the Parish of St Augustine of Canterbury, Whitton.

With many congratulations and my prayers for this year of celebration.

+ George Cantuar

ARCHBISHOP OF CANTERBURY

Acknowledgements

It is my privilege to thank the individuals and institutions who offered guidance, encouragement, and practical assistance during the production of this book. Thanks are due to The British Museum, English Heritage, Corpus Christi College, Cambridge, and the Dean and Chapter of Canterbury Cathedral who allowed me to use illustrations from their collections. I am especially grateful to Brother Aidan, The Hermitage of Saints Anthony and Cuthbert, who sent me his own exquisite painting of St Augustine, and to Father Silouan, Community of St John the Baptist, who drew my attention to some of the important but less well known events in the history of the Old English Church. Professionals who have been generous with their time and ideas include Nick Hillman, who designed the book, and Madeleine Swann, who compiled the index. I received encouragement, inspiration, and support from my family and from Father Rod Cosh, vicar of the Parish of St Augustine of Canterbury, Whitton, who conceived the idea for the book.

Carole Reeves
Richmond, Surrey
December 1996

Introduction

'How then are they to call on him if they have not come to believe in him? And how can they believe in him if they have never heard of him? And how will they hear of him unless there is a preacher for them? And how will there be preachers if they are not sent? As scripture says: How beautiful are the feet of the messenger of good news.'

Romans 10: 14, 15

On a clear afternoon in the spring of the year 597, a tall windswept soldier paced the narrow sandspit which projected into the sea at Ebbsfleet harbour on the Kentish Isle of Thanet. To its inhabitants, the word Thanet meant 'bright island' for it was here that the Romans had built a lighthouse.[1] At that time, Thanet was a true island separated from mainland Kent by the sweet waters of the River Wantsum which was about three-eighths of a mile wide and could be crossed in only two places.[2] From his vantage point looking south east towards the great Continent of Europe, the soldier would have the first sighting of an invasion from the sea, and his keen eyes scanned the bleak horizon for miniscule blots of movement which might foreshadow a raid by Saxon pirates or herald the arrival of a fleet of trading vessels. Across the narrow estuary where the Wantsum flowed into the sea, he could see the massive stone walls of the old fort at Richborough. The fort was already several centuries old for it, too, had been built by the Romans long before the soldier's own ancestors had crossed the North Sea to settle in Britain. He shivered as the chilly April gusts whipped the sea spray into his face, and pulled his sheepskin cloak tightly around his shoulders.

During his watch as one of the guardians of the Saxon Shore, the soldier's attention was occasionally diverted by the scrunch of scraping pebbles followed by a raw jubilant shout which echoed across the tidal flat. Looking up, he would smile to see a

---

1 Phillips, Father Andrew. *Orthodox Christianity and the Old English Church.* Greenprint & Design in association with The English Orthodox Trust, 1996: p 7.
2 Bede. *Ecclesiastical History.* Ed Colgrave B, Mynors R A B. Clarendon Press, Oxford 1991: i.25.

dog racing across the shingle followed by a roughly clad Jutish boy brandishing a forked stick hung with game. His eyes would follow the boy as he zigzagged his way along the wild Kentish beach to disappear into the fringe of forest which rimmed the curve of the harbour. From these tightly packed oak, ash, yew and birch trees arose several wispy spirals of smoke, suggestive of rude hamlets and hunters' camps. The soldier would spend some minutes imagining the boy's homecoming amongst the woodland folk before returning his gaze towards the Gallic port of Boulogne-sur-Mer from where a ship carrying an important party from Rome had been expected for several weeks. His liege lord, King Aethelberht of Kent, had commanded immediate word of the arrival of such a ship for it was rumoured that those who travelled in her had powers greater than ordinary men. The king himself had foretold that the visitors would be preceded by a sign from heaven.

The soldier's watch was nearly over when he spied far out, in a sea turning to twilight, a thirty-oared boat curved in prow and stem, while winging across the sky, a flock of marsh birds made their evening flight towards the undrained inlets of the Thanet estuary. His instinct told him that King Aethelberht's prophecy had been fulfilled.

Within a short time, a small crowd had gathered at the harbour, all listening keenly for the familiar slap of the waves against a wooden hull and the creak of oars pulling in weary unison as the rowers strained the final yards to the beach. Inside the boat, men were singing; not the lusty rowing shanties so beloved of seafarers returning from a voyage, but a strange melodic chant which captivated its listeners as a sound foreign to their ears. Two of the king's arms bearers waded into the water to greet the leader of the party whom his companions named as Father Augustine. It so happened that in the act of disembarking, Father Augustine slipped upon a stone which, to the wonder of the onlookers, took the imprint of his foot even as mud and clay would have done. The stone was immediately taken up and carried with all honour to a small chapel nearby.[3]

---

3   This story was related by Thorne, a fourteenth century monk and chronicler of St Augustine's Abbey. Some remains of the chapel was said to have existed in the time of Henry VIII and were shown by an old hermit to the antiquary, John Leland, who made a tour through England between 1535 and 1543, searching monastic and collegiate libraries for old authors.

The two centuries between the fall of the Roman Empire in 410 and the arrival of St Augustine are known in Britain as the Dark Ages. They were dark because they were devoid of the influence of civilisation, being neither Roman nor yet medieval. They were dark because the inhabitants of Britain were illiterate and left few records of their existence or achievements. They were dark because the light of Christianity had not penetrated the hearts and minds of the pagan population.

All of these things are true but do not tell the whole story of this important period in the history of the people of Britain. Roman civilisation did not disappear from the island overnight because all freeborn Britons were also Roman citizens. At the same time, British society was never wholly Roman since large sections of its population were never influenced by Roman culture. The Picts, Scots, Irish and Welsh retained their own identities throughout Roman occupation and made important contributions to later European thought. Many of them had already been converted to Christianity in the Celtic tradition. The Saxon invaders who arrived when Roman society was on the wane brought their own values and ideas which although inspired by pagan mythology, were nonetheless influential in establishing the first laws of the land.

The Dark Ages represent a challenge to historians who are forced to sift the few remaining contemporary sources to separate the facts from the myths and legends. Nevertheless, the legends have had important consequences for history even into our own time. It was the Dark Ages which produced the legend of King Arthur whose Christian values created the model of a golden age of good government in which the weak were protected from barbarism without and oppression within. The belief that Arthur would come again urged chivalrous restraint upon the crude authority of arbitrary rulers and gave courage to their subjects to struggle for a just and free society of peace and ease.[4] Each retelling of the tale clothed Arthur in the ideas and

---

4   Morris J R. The literary evidence. In Barley M W, Hanson R P C (eds). *Christianity in Britain, 300-700.* Leicester University Press, 1968.

morals of its own day. It was also the Dark Ages which gave rise to the great monastic movement which began in south Wales and spread to Ireland, Northumbria, Gaul, and central Europe. Britain was, in fact, the principal point of origin of the monasteries of later medieval Europe.

Much of our knowledge of the Dark Ages comes from written sources which were compiled by scholars who lived afterwards. The Anglo-Saxon Chronicles[5] were probably begun in the ninth century, and the Venerable Bede's Ecclesiastical History [6] was completed in 731. There are, nevertheless, important contemporary documents from the fifth and sixth centuries which were written by monastic scholars such as Gildas who observed events at home, and also by Britons living abroad.

The story of St Augustine's mission to Britain cannot begin with his arrival in Kent since the circumstances which brought him to these shores are to be found in the history of the people for several centuries beforehand. But who were the British people? How did they live? What sort of island did Augustine find in 597? How did the Christianity which he preached differ from that which was already rooted in British soil? What was his mission? Was it successful and how was it achieved? What were the long term consequences of the mission? This book does not promise to provide all the answers to these intriguing questions but, hopefully, it will help set the scene for those interested enough to make their own pilgrimage to the places where, fourteen hundred years ago, St Augustine of Canterbury and his missionaries established what was to become the Church of England.

5   An illustrated translation of the Anglo-Saxon Chronicles by Anne Savage, with historical commentary, is published by Phoebe Phillips in association with William Heinemann, London 1982.

6   There are several versions of Bede's *Ecclesiastic History* available including a Penguin Classics edition. I have used the Oxford Medieval Texts edition (reference 2) which contains the Latin original alongside a translation, with excellent historical commentary.

Anglo-Saxon England

Chapter 1
St Augustine's Journey

'Look, I am sending you out like sheep among wolves; so be cunning as snakes and yet innocent as doves.'

St Matthew 10: 16

Early in the sixth century, a Roman nobleman named Benedict of Nursia, founded a monastery at Monte Cassino, between Rome and Naples. One of Benedict's most ardent disciples was the influential Christian teacher, Gregory the Great, who built the Benedictine monastery of St Andrew at Monte Celio in Rome. One day, in the late 570s, Gregory noticed a group of fair-skinned pagan youths in the Roman slave market and was told that they were *Angli* who came from the island of Britain.[1] To the compassionate and pious Gregory, the fair-skinned *Angli* had 'the faces of angels, and such men should be fellow- heirs of the angels in heaven.'[2] The prophetic significance of his encounter was further intensified when he learned from the boys themselves that they came from the Northumbrian province of Deira which was ruled by King Aelle. Gregory thereby pronounced that the boys would be rescued *De ira Dei* (from the wrath of God), and that their land would echo the praise of God in *Alleluia*. Out of this remarkable incident was conceived the mission which Gregory nurtured for a further twenty years.

In Britain at this time, the Anglian people were grouped into two large and powerful realms with the River Humber forming their natural boundary. In Northumbria, King Aelle of Deira died in 588 and his kingdom was acquired by Aethelric of Bernicia who, for the first time, united the peoples of the north into a single kingdom.

---

1 This story has been made familiar by Bede in his *Ecclesiastical History* (completed AD 731). However, there is an earlier version preserved in *The earliest life of Gregory the Great by an anonymous monk of Whitby.* Ed B Colgrave. University of Kansas, 1968: pp 90-93. Cited in Stenton, Sir F. *Anglo-Saxon England. The Oxford History of England.* Third edition, Oxford University Press 1985: p 103.

2 Bede. *Ecclesiastical History*: ii.1

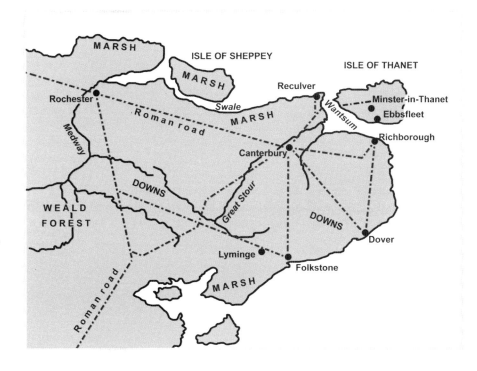

Anglo-Saxon Kent

Aethelric's son, Aethelfirth, married King Aelle's daughter and is remembered as a heroic warrior and the first great leader of the northern Angles.[3] The land south of the Humber and east of the Severn was more populous, more diverse, and divided into many kingdoms, most of which were very small. Here, in a land where populations were more mobile, society was generally less stable, kingdoms were insecure, and allegiances shifted in tune with frequent dynastic upheavals.

The Kingdom of Kent was the wealthiest, most independent and civilised of the southern kingdoms and was Britain's bridge to the Continent. For many years, Britain had been an important source of slaves which appear to have been traded by Frisian[4] merchants acting as middlemen between the Rhineland and Kent. In return for this human commerce, Kent received luxury goods such as weapons, jewellry, glass-ware, wine and gold from the Mediterranean, and garnets and spices from the Far East.[5] Kent had a ruling dynasty going back more than a century and it was on these foundations that King Aethelberht of Kent won and held for more than twenty years the title *Bretwalda* which gave him suzerainty over all the Angles of the south.[6] Aethelberht was at the height of his power by the time that Aethelfirth succeeded the Northumbrian throne in 593, and for the next twenty-three years (both kings died in 616), the whole of Britain south of the River Clyde was overshadowed by the two great Anglian kings.[7]

The distinctive social and political structure of Kent owed much to Continental, particularly Frankish influence and there is no doubt that there were close commercial and cultural links between the two kingdoms. Before he succeeded to the Kentish throne in 560, Aethelberht had married a Frankish princess, Bertha, the daughter of Charibert, king of Paris. Bertha's ancestor was the great Clovis, Christian ruler of the Franks, who in 486, captured the Roman province of Gaul. Gaul became France and the Franks dominated central Europe. Aethelberht's marriage into the great

---

3   Stenton, Sir F. *Op cit:* p 73-79.

4   Frisia corresponds to an area which includes modern day Holland. See chapter 2.

5   Witney K P. *The Kingdom of Kent.* Phillimore, London & Chicester 1982: p 80.

6   The term *Bretwalda* literally means `Britain Ruler' and was the title given to a war leader or supreme commander who could call on the support of other kingdoms. Witney K P. *Op cit:* p 47, 91.

7   Morris J. *The age of Arthur: A history of the British Isles from 350 to 650.* Weidenfeld & Nicolson, London 1984: p 239.

St Martin's Church, Canterbury. Queen Bertha and her household worshipped here before the arrival of St Augustine. It is England's oldest parish church and was built over the ruins of a Romano-British church. Tradition has it that the font dates to the time of King Aethelberht's baptism. (Photograph by the author)

The Queningate in the east wall of the City of Canterbury was used by Queen Bertha as she walked to St Martin's Church. (Photograph by the author)

Merovingian dynasty established by Clovis, brought Kent into the sphere of influence of the Roman church although Aethelberht, as pagan ruler of a small kingdom, would not have been regarded as an equal to the Frankish kings.[8] In their policy of expansion, the Franks owed much to the Catholic bishops of Gaul, and Bertha came to Kent with a retinue which included Luithard, bishop of Senlis, as her chaplain. Queen Bertha and her household worshipped just outside the walls of Canterbury in a small chapel which had been built during the Roman occupation by a Romano-British chieftain named Lucius, and dedicated to the Virgin Mary.[9] Bertha restored it and had it reconsecrated to St Martin of Tours.[10] Although she never succeeded in converting her husband, Bertha's influence during their long marriage undoubtedly had a significant effect on the environment which made Aethelberht receptive to Christianity.

> `and if a woman has a husband who is not a believer and he is willing to stay with her, she should not divorce her husband. You see, the unbelieving husband is sanctified through his wife and the unbelieving wife is sanctified through the brother. If this were not so, your children would be unclean, whereas in fact they are holy. '
>
> I Corinthians 7: 13,14

Gregory the Great became Pope Gregory I in 590 and within five years he had organised, through a priest in Gaul named Candidus, the purchase of Anglian slave boys who were educated in monasteries in readiness for a mission to Britain. As leader of the mission, Gregory chose Augustine, the prior of his own monastery of St Andrew and a personal friend and confidant. Augustine had been a student of Bishop Felix of Messina, in Sicily, before joining the monastery on Monte Celio where, in the early days, he had shared a cell with Gregory himself.[11] He had probably also accompanied Gregory to Constantinople in 579 when the former was appointed Papal legate

---

8   Stenton, Sir F. *Op cit:* p 59.
9   Phillips, Father Andrew. *Op cit:* p 8.
10 For Martin of Tours see chapter 3.
11 Donaldson C. *In the footsteps of St Augustine. The great English pilgrimage from Rome to Canterbury: 1400th anniversary AD597-1997.* The Canterbury Press, Norwich 1995: p 19.

to the Imperial Court.[12] Augustine was a tall man with a commanding presence and is said to have been haughty and rather pompous whilst remaining loyal and sub-servient to his ecclesiastical superiors. He was a shrewd and cautious diplomat rather than an individualist, and these were exactly the qualities which Gregory would have known so well and deemed so appropriate for such an important and delicate mission.

The mission set out from Rome some time after August 595. Before it left, Pope Gregory blessed the assembled missionaries as they stood in his lofty monastery for the last time, looking down upon the still magnificent city of Rome, golden in the late summer sun.[13] The priests and monks sailed from the port of Ostia to the monastic island of Lérins in southern Gaul where they were warmly received by the abbot, Stephen. At some point in southern Gaul, the mission halted because of the extreme reluctance of some of its members to confront the barbarians of Britain whose sav-age character and coarse, unwritten language was so alien to the high-minded culture of Rome. Augustine duly returned to Rome to request release from the mission.

It is likely that only part of this story is accurate and that, in reality, the Pope's emissary was insufficiently provided with written authority commending the mission to the Frankish kings and ecclesiastical leaders in Gaul. Perhaps Augustine's own authority over his companions had also been imprecisely defined.[14] Whatever the rea-son for the interruption of the mission, it was henceforth given full papal sanction through a series of letters, dated 23 July 596, which Gregory addressed to those individuals whose support he considered important for the mission's success.[15] Amongst these was a letter of encouragement to Augustine's companions reinforc-ing his appointment as their abbot. Other letters were addressed to the Merovingian kings, Theudrich of Burgundy and Theudebert of Austrasia, and their grandmother,

---

12 Phillips, Father Andrew. *Op cit:* p 2.

13 This site is today marked with a plaque to commemorate the beginning of the mission to Britain. *Ibid:* p 20.

14 Stenton, Sir F. *Op cit:* p 105.

15 These letters survive and remain the fundamental authorities for the mission of Augustine. They are collected in Haddan A W, Stubbs W (eds). *Councils and Ecclesiastical Documents relating to Great Britain and Ireland.* Vol iii, Oxford 1871. Cited in Stenton, Sir F. *Op cit:* p 704.

Queen Brunhild. The diplomatic phrasing of these papal documents gives the impression that the Merovingian kings were overlords of the pagan *Angli*, and in paternalistic fashion, desired their conversion to the Christian faith. However, there is a suggestion that King Aethelberht was prepared for a mission and that earlier contacts with the church in Gaul had come to nothing. He may even have sent word to Rome directly rather than approach the Merovingian kings who were more than likely to attach political conditions to any religious assistance.[16] Pope Gregory's involvement in the initiation of the mission was also extremely important. He became pope at a time when there were fierce disputes over primacy between Rome and Constantinople which compromised the authority of the Church. Gregory's own mandate was to claim authority for Catholic Christianity in the west where churches were beginning to be governed with little reference to Rome.[17] Amongst the British, the monastic movement was becoming a mighty force but it was influenced by the austere piety of the Irish monks rather than the ostentation of the Roman Church.[18] Increasing numbers of ascetic Irish and British monks were making the short sea crossing to Gaul and the Rhineland and were bringing a new and incalculable element into Continental religious life.

At Arles, in southern Gaul, sometime between July and September 596, Augustine was consecrated bishop[19], and by the time that he and his companions had travelled northwards through Lyons, Tours, and Paris, the group was forty strong, having been joined by individuals such as the young Anglian missionaries rescued from slavery by the priest, Candidus. They journeyed at a leisurely pace and would have had no difficulty passing the nights comfortably as guests at one or other

---

16 Wallace-Hadrill J M. *Early Germanic kingship in England and on the Continent* (1971). Cited in Witney K P. *Op cit:* p 111.

17 Following his meeting with the young slaves in the market, Gregory requested the then Pope (Benedict I) that he be sent to Britain to convert the *Angli*. The Pope was willing but Gregory's popularity was such that the citizens of Rome refused to allow him to leave. Bede. *Ecclesiastical History:* ii.1.

18 For the rise of the monastic movement in Britain see chapter 3.

19 Bede wrote that Augustine returned to Arles to be consecrated after his arrival in Kent. However, a letter written by Gregory in July 598 to Eulogius, patriarch of Alexandria, of which Bede apparently did not know, suggests that Augustine was consecrated at Arles before he reached Kent. This would make more sense. See footnote 1 in Bede. *Ecclesiastical History:* i.27.

of the two hundred monasteries which lined their route through the land of the Franks.[20] The missionaries spent most of the winter in Paris and did not cross the channel into Kent until after Easter which in 597 fell on 13 April.[21] It was several days before King Aethelberht, accompanied by the notables of his kingdom, arrived on the isle of Thanet to meet the Pope's emissaries. In the interim, he supplied them with food and other necessities but would not allow them to leave the island. There is a tradition that Queen Bertha visited Augustine prior to her husband's official reception of the missionaries. There was formerly a stone in the church at Minster-in-Thanet where Augustine is reputed to have sat in conversation with the Queen.[22]

The meeting with Aethelberht took place under the open sky because, according to legend, the king and his retainers were afraid of the strangers' magic.[23] At the king's command, the missionaries sat and 'preached the word of life' to all who were present. Then Aethelberht said to them:

> 'The words and the promises you bring are fair enough, but because they are new to us and doubtful, I cannot consent to accept them and forsake those beliefs which I and the whole English race have held so long. But as you have come on a long pilgrimage and are anxious, I perceive, to share with us things which you believe to be true and good, we do not wish to do you harm; on the contrary, we will receive you hospitably and provide what is necessary for your support; nor do we forbid you to win all you can to your faith and religion by your preaching.'[24]

20 Matthew D. *Atlas of Medieval Europe.* BCA, London 1983: p 45.
21 Phillips, Father Andrew. *Op cit:* p 6.
22 *Ibid:* p 9.
23 It was also customary at this time for meetings to be held outside. Witney K P. *Op cit:* p 111. It is unlikely that the missionaries would have frightened Aethelberht who was accustomed to a Christian household but his companions, drawn from the Kentish aristocracy, may have harboured distrust. The outside meeting may have been arranged to allay their suspicions.
24 Bede. *Ecclesiastical History:* i.25.

Carrying a great silver cross brought from Rome and a holy icon of Jesus Christ, Augustine led the missionaries on the final stage of their long journey to Canterbury where they arrived, probably, on 25 April. In unison they sang as they walked:

> 'We beseech Thee, O Lord, in Thy great mercy, that Thy wrath and anger may
> be turned away from this city and from Thy holy house, for we have sinned.
> Alleluia.[25]

They were provided with a dwelling-place in the area known as Stablegate to the north of the city. Augustine is said to have held his first Canterbury mass in an old Roman church which had been long used by King Aethelberht and his household as a pagan temple.[26] Augustine reconsecrated it to St Pancras,[27,28] and he may have had sentimental reasons for doing this since a church dedicated to this saint stood on Monte Celio near to his own monastery.

If the initiative which inspired the Augustinian mission was partly the responsibility of King Aethelberht, why was its fulfilment so prolonged? After all, the king had been married to a pious Christian princess for almost forty years. The probable answer is that the time and circumstances were not right beforehand and that it was the winning of the *Bretwaldship* which may have brought into focus for Aethelberht the model of a supreme ruler who aspired to be something more than a war leader.[29]

25 *Ibid.* This prayer belongs to the Gallican Liturgy and was used as an antiphon during Rogation Day processions. These processions before Ascension Day were not used in Rome at this time. Augustine may have learned the practice on his journey through Gaul.

26 According to Thorne, the fourteenth century chronicler of St Augustine's Abbey.

27 St Pancras was a young Greek who was martyred at the time of the Emperor Diocletian (284-305) whose persecution of the Christians began in 303. The martyr's family had owned the land on Monte Celio on which the monastery of St Andrew had been built. Godfrey J. *The Church in Anglo-Saxon England.* Cambridge University Press, 1962: p 78.

28 Phillips, Father Andrew. *Op cit:* p 13.

29 Witney K P. *Op cit:* p 113.

St Pancras Chapel was believed to have been a pagan temple consecrated by St Augustine. The remains of the small south chapel to the right of the chancel (rebuilt c 1390) is revered as the site of his first mass in Canterbury. (Photograph by the author)

In an age when people lived close to the natural world, it was not easy to make the transition from paganism, with its belief that the gods existed in the forces of nature, to Christian monotheism which held that nature was subservient to man and that God created the world as something apart from Himself.[30,31] This was not a literate but a bardic society and the pagan cults were fired with magic and poetry, part of a complex of traditions from Norse and German mythology which united the Angli in a sense of shared values and a common heroic past based on the power of individual might. A whole philosophy of life was bound up in these beliefs and they were not abandoned until the Angli, like other barbarian tribes who accepted Christianity, perceived that might did not necessarily equate with right. Faith that God would prevail over injustice gave men strength to endure hardship and violence at a time when there was no powerful law and state to restore right. The earth was the centre of God's universe and the Church was his faithful community. The aspirations to strive for earthly power and glory were weakened since these would all too quickly disappear in death. In God's eyes, all men were equal, and with idealism focused on God as the only acknowledged sovereign, people began to believe that they could appeal to him with confidence to intervene in their affairs.

30 For an appreciation of how people viewed their place in the natural world, read Keith Thomas. *Man and the natural world: changing attitudes in England 1500-1800.* Penguin Books, 1984. Whilst the period covered is much later and clearly influenced by Christianity, the philosophy is much closer to the Dark Ages than to our own time.

31 God blessed them, saying to them, 'Be fruitful, multiply, fill the earth and subdue it. Be masters of the fish of the sea, the birds of heaven and all the living creatures that move on earth.' Genesis 1: 28.

Chapter2
The People of Dark Age Britain

`If you go into your neighbour's vineyard, you may eat as many grapes as you please, but you must not put any in your basket. '

Deuteronomy 23: 25

Julius Caesar was the first Roman commander to cross the channel into Britain from Gaul. He made two expeditions between 54 and 55 BC but it was to be a further century before the Emperor Claudius arrived at the head of an invasion force (which included an elephant corps), with the sole purpose of subjugating the barbarian British tribes. This he pursued with such unrelenting ferocity that it led to the bloody rebellion, in AD 60-61, of Boudicca, ruler of the Iceni tribe of East Anglia.

Between Claudius' invasion and the end of the fourth century, however, Roman rule brought both an increase in the numbers and in the material prosperity of the population. The Romans brought political stability to the warring, hostile tribes, expanded markets, developed a monetary economy, exploited natural resources such as forests, mines and quarries, and built new towns, roads, forts, country houses and ports.[1] Britain exported corn to feed the Roman armies on the Rhine; raw materials, especially lead and tin; and manufactured goods such as textiles whose price was regulated by Imperial Edict. By the beginning of the fourth century, much of Britain's natural woodland had been cleared because considerable amounts of timber were required for building, domestic heating, and as fuel for manufacturing processes. Deforestation was also equated with civilisation since forests were perceived as wild and dangerous places, homes for animals rather than people.[2]

---

1   Myres J N L. *The English settlements: The Oxford History of England.* Oxford University Press, 1986: p 202ff.
2   Thomas Keith. *Op cit:* chapter 5.

All freeborn inhabitants of Britain were Roman citizens and the chief threats to their economic and social stability came from the barbarian tribes beyond the borders of their control. These included the Picts, the tattooed people of northern Britain beyond the River Forth,[3] and the Saxon pirates who mounted increasingly destructive coastal raids. The Romans never subdued the Picts, against whose fierce, insistent attacks they built the Hadrian and Antonine walls. Barbarian invasions from the sea threatened the eastern lowlands of Britain from the early years of the third century, and by about 275, a series of coastal fortresses were built on an arc from the Wash to Southampton Water, and placed under the command of the Count of the Saxon Shore. The main fortress was at Richborough which was also the headquarters of a fleet.[4,5] Most of the invasions were by small `hit and run' units, but during the fourth century there was considerable settlement into the lowlands of `ocean peoples' who were predominantly of Germanic stock and included Angles, Jutes, Frisians, and Saxons. The Saxon Shore itself was defended by German mercenaries, or *laeti*, as well as Roman troops, and it is likely that many *laeti* became integrated into the Romano-British community.

The Dark Ages are marked as the period of great migration of peoples westward across Asia and Europe, when the frontiers of the Roman Empire were being continuously assailed by previously settled tribes evicted from their homelands. On 24 August 410, the Visigoths, a Germanic tribe which had been forced to flee from the Balkans by the devastating invasion of the Asiatic Huns, entered and sacked the City of Rome, bringing the thousand year history of classical civilisation to an ignominious end. From his monastery in Bethlehem, St Jerome wept, but younger men saw the destruction of Rome as an opportunity to build a new society.

---

3   They were called Picts because *pictus* is the Latin for `tattooed'.
4   Witney K P. *Op cit:* p 9.
5   Myres J N L. *Op cit:* p 91.

A British monk living in Siciliy wrote:

'You tell me that everyone is saying that the world is coming to an end. So what? It happened before. Remember Noah's time ... But after the Flood, men were holier.'[6]

In Britain, the Roman way of life was maintained for a generation or so by wealthy landowners in the lowlands, particularly in the Cotswolds, where the rural economy was surprisingly resilient despite Rome's increasing political weakness. In the poorer areas such as Dumnonia (Devon and Cornwall), Demetia (Pembroke and Carmarthen), central and northern Wales, landowners were humbler men who were nearer to their tenants in interest and outlook. Here, the breakdown in Roman culture occurred much more rapidly. Before the middle of the fifth century, both the Roman military and civilian administrations disappeared from Britain.[7] Trade was disrupted by barbarian pirates, and the previously good relations between the *laeti* and German settlers began to founder. These immigrants maintained contact with their kin amongst the restless tribes beyond the North Sea and waited for the dust to settle.

Meanwhile, the native Britons lost their Roman identity and called themselves *combrogi* meaning the 'fellow-countrymen'. Modern forms are *Cymry* in Welsh and *Cumber* in English. The immigrants knew them by both names and added a third, calling them 'foreigners'; *wealh* or *wylisc* in Old English, *Welsh* in modern English. They also adopted a general collective name for themselves which was *Engle* or *Englisc*, written in Latin as *Angli*. Angles, Jutes, Frisians, Saxons and Scandinavians all called themselves *Angli* or English when they settled in Britain and were all described as Saxons by their British neighbours.[8]

6   Quoted in Morris J. *Op cit:* p 23.
7   Morris J R. The literary evidence. In Barley M W, Hanson R P C (eds).
8   Eighth century Continental writers devised the term *Angli Saxones* to distinguish the Saxons of Britain from those of Germany. Morris J. *Op cit:* p 42.

The homelands of the English settlers.

In 425, a British aristocrat from a wealthy family of Cotswold landowners, was elected to power in the Roman tradition and probably held the title of emperor. His name was Vortigern,[9] meaning 'overking'. Within three years of Vortigern's election, lowland Britain was seriously threatened by an invasion of Picts who took to the sea in order to bypass the northern military defences, sailing down the east coast towards Norfolk. As a defensive measure, Vortigern invited into Britain a Jutish expeditionary force of about a hundred men under their exceptionally bold and able war leader, Hengest the Dane.[10] Hengest's warriors landed at Ebbsfleet in three strong keels propelled by oars. The threatened invasion was successfully forestalled and the Jutes were billeted on the Isle of Thanet. Hengest is said to have persuaded Vortigern to allow him to send for reinforcements so that, within a short time, there arrived a further forty keels carrying most of Hengest's kin including his brother, Horsa, and their strongest sailors. This awesome armada travelled in convoy as far as northern Britain where it routed the Picts and plundered the Orkneys before splitting up and landing at strategic sites along the east coast.[11] Vortigern's fateful invitation to the barbarians of Jutland[12] saved Britain from becoming Pictland in the short term, but in the long term it was to turn southern Britain into England.[13]

Hengest sealed his alliance with Vortigern by giving him his daughter in marriage. In return he asked for the district of Kent which Vortigern granted, expelling the existing British ruler, Gwyrangon.[14] Canterbury is the only city in Britain which the Saxon invaders are said to have acquired by treaty rather than by conquest. It is also the only city where there is evidence of Saxon living side by side with the last of the Romans. Hengest's control of Kent and the eastern shoreline opened the floodgates to Saxon settlement. Gildas, a British priest, writing a century after the invasion, described how:

9   As was usual with British notables, Vortigern bore a Latin name, Vitalis or Vitalinus, as well as his title. *Ibid*: p 55.

10   The Danes were the greatest seafarers of the age.

11   *The Kentish Chronicle*. Cited in Morris J. *Op cit*: p 61.

12   There is some controversy amongst scholars as to whether the Jutes were natives of Jutland or whether they came from the area around the lower Rhine. See Witney K P. *Op cit*: p 14ff; Morris J. *Op cit*: p 261ff; Myres J N L. *Op cit*: p 46ff; Stenton Sir F. *Op cit*: p 14ff.

13   Pictland became Scotland in the ninth century when an Irish Scot dynasty (Scot was the Latin name for the Irish) secured the throne of Pictland. Morris J. *Op cit*: 42.

14   Gwyrangon was a native Briton and probably a Christian. *Kentish Chronicle*. Cited in Morris J. *Op cit*: 74.

`... All the greater towns fell to the enemy's battering rams; all their inhabitants, bishops, priests and people, were mown down together, while swords flashed and flames crackled ... there was no burial save in the ruins of the houses, or in the bellies of the beasts and birds.'[15]

In those towns where urban society was maintained, it existed only at subsistence level, even to the end of the fifth century. In the countryside, most of the Roman country houses, villas and farms were abandoned to ruin with very few being taken over by Saxon squatters. Wide tracts of lowland which had been cleared of forest and brought into cultivation reverted to wilderness, waste and scrub. Many Britons fled to the Armorican peninsula in Gaul, which had long been abandoned by the Romans. By the middle of the sixth century, the peninsula was entirely British and was called *Britannia minor* (Lesser Britain) by Gregory the Great. It later became known as Brittany.[16]

By about 442, Britain was largely under Saxon control. The worst destruction occurred in the eastern and central lowlands which were the wealthiest, most densely populated, and most highly civilised regions of Roman Britain. In the north and west, where native culture had been less softened by Roman influence, the British were more resilient, retaining their own languages, cultures, and social structures even from pre-Roman times.[17] It was in these areas that Christianity became a powerful unifying force and a continuing reminder of spiritual links with Gaul, Rome, and the Mediterranean.[18]

Hengest's invaders probably encountered little resistance from most British communities. The population of lowland Britain at this time was only about a million,[19] and it is likely that Hengest could muster a crack fighting force of up to two thousand men.[20] Apart from battering rams which Gildas mentions, the Saxons

15 Gildas. *De Excidio Britanniae*. Quoted in *ibid*: p 74.
16 Morris J. *Op cit*: p 254.
17 Wroxeter, for example, remained British for a further two hundred years. *Ibid*: p 75.
18 For the rise of Christianity in Britain, see chapter 3.
19 Myres J N L. *Op cit*: p 44.
20 Witney K P. *Op cit*: 68.

were well armed with thrusting spears and wooden shields with heavy iron bosses. They probably also carried stabbing knives. A particularly vicious and typically Frankish weapon was the *francisca*, or throwing axe. The Jutish contingent, under Frankish influence, also used bows and arrows. Neither the Saxons nor the Britons wore body armour, but whereas the former were foot soldiers, the latter did have some cavalry forces.[21] The horse was said to be unknown to the Saxons although this is unlikely since the name Hengest means 'stallion'.[22]

Sometime between 449 and 453, the British appealed for help against the Saxon marauders to Aetius, the Roman commander in Gaul. The appeal went unanswered because Aetius was faced with the threat of Attila and the Huns as well as the relentless westward movement of the Franks.

❋ ❋ ❋ ❋ ❋

After the first wave of invasion, most of the immigrants who followed came as settlers rather than as soldiers. They were part of the mass movement of peoples westward from Russia and Asia across the Mediterranean and European world. By the end of the fifth century, encroachment of the Franks, Danes, and Slavs into Germanic lands once inhabited by Jutes, Angles, Saxons, and Frisians made continuing tenure all but impossible. They came to Britain because they were squeezed out of Europe. The British, however, were united in fear and hatred of the newcomers who were obliged to rally together under the superior numbers of a nation whose government and state they had destroyed but whose will to resist was not yet crushed. By the 480s, the Saxon expansion was blocked by the British but they lived securely enough in small agricultural communities, each developing a class of notables. In Kent, the lands inherited from Hengest's marriage treaty with Vortigern were among the

---

21 The stirrup, however, was unknown at this time.

22 Procopius of Caesarea, wrote in the mid-sixth century, that horses were unknown to the Saxons. Cited in Witney K P. *Op cit:* p 44; Stenton, Sir F. *Op cit:* p 4ff. One of the reasons which scholars give for the unlikely existence of Hengest's brother, Horsa, is that the word means 'gelding', an unlikely epithet for a Danish warrior.

richest in Britain. Hengest himself was succeeded by Oeric, surnamed Oesc, who founded the Kentish royal house known as the Oescingas.[23]

The siege of Mons Badonicus (Mount Badon) in about 500, was the last attempt by the British to restore the Roman civilisation into which they had been born.[24] Oesc of Kent is the only Saxon king known to have fought at Badon and he would have witnessed, with a mixture of awe and despair, the legendary Arthur lead a fierce cavalry charge in which nearly a thousand of his own countrymen were slaughtered.[25] Badon was the final victory for the British after which there was relative peace for forty years. At about this time, Oesc became the father of a son whom he named Eormenric after the legendary king of the Ostrogoths, a mighty warrior who, more than a century before, had conquered a vast empire from the Baltic to the Black Sea. Eormenric of Kent was the father of King Aethelberht.

'The old order changeth, yielding place to new,

And God fulfils himself in many ways,

Lest one good custom should corrupt the world.

Comfort thyself: what comfort is in me?

I have lived my life, and that which I have done

May He within himself make pure! but thou

If thou shouldst never see my face again,

Pray for my soul. More things are wrought by prayer

Than this world dreams of.'[26]

---

23 According to Bede (ii.5), Oesc was Hengest's son but this is disputed by some historians who consider him to the son of Hengest's captain in Bernicia whom Hengest named as his heir. Morris J. *Op cit:* p 272.

24 The site of the siege has not been conclusively identified. Some historians opt for Bath (Morris J. *Op cit:* p 112) while others have suggested Badbury where there is a pre-Roman hill fort, or Baydon which at 760 feet above sea level, is the most elevated village in Wiltshire. Myres J N L. *Op cit:* p 159.

25 King Arthur's existence remains a point of contention among scholars. In his account of the British siege of *Mons Badonicus,* Gildas mentions only the leader, Ambrosius Aurelianus. The evidence for Arthur's contribution rests with the ninth century Welsh scholar, Nennius, who wrote that *Mons Badonicus* was Arthur's twelfth and final victory.

26 Tennyson. *Morte d'Arthur.*

The golden age of peace which followed Arthur's victory at Badon, and which produced the Arthurian legend, was brought to an end not by Arthur's death at the hand of Mordred, but by bubonic plague which began in Egypt in about 541 and reached Constantinople two years later. The plague travelled in trade ships to south west Britain, Ireland, and the land of the Picts.[27] It devastated both the British and the Irish but not the Saxons who had no dealings with their British neighbours. In addition, they traded with northern Gaul which was also spared. A contemporary writer observed that:

`... Plague favours war and does not harm the rough races ...'[28]

an observation which might equally have been applied to the heathen Saxons as it was applied, in this case, to the Moors of north Africa.

In the aftermath of plague came a Saxon uprising in which settlers infiltrated and colonised the enfeebled communities of Somerset, the Cotswolds, Cirencester, southern Britain and the south midlands. In 568, King Aethelberht attempted a power push beyond his ancestral borders with the possible objective of controlling London, the chief town of the East Saxons. The bid was unsuccessful so Aethelberht sought an alternative to power through aggression by marrying his sister, Ricula, to Sledda, king of the East Saxons. In this way, Essex became a virtual dependency of Kent. Whether Aethelberht later won the *Bretwaldship* through force of arms is unknown but it was as a protector rather than a conqueror and a plunderer that he maintained it. If the role of the *Bretwalda* was to be an arbiter among kings rather than a war leader, it needed a strong moral authority behind it. Whatever other influences may have been working upon Aethelberht before he won his supremacy, its achievement may have been the decisive factor which turned him towards Christianity.

27 Modern day Scotland
28 Quoted in Morris J. *Op cit:* p 223.

Chapter 3
Christianity in Dark Age Britain

`Well then, I say, is it possible that they have not heard? Indeed they have: in the entire earth their voice stands out, their message reaches the whole world.'

Romans 10: 18

Christianity made its first impact upon the peoples of the Latin west in Italy and Africa; but in Gaul and Britain, Christians remained few and insignificant. Alban of Verulamium,[1] executed in 209, is the earliest known Latin Christian of the European provinces but in a world demoralised by submission to authority, a faith which men held dearer than life commanded respect. Christians themselves claimed that every martyr made ten converts. Orthodox Christian teaching emphasised that salvation was the prerogative of the poor and humble; that wealth and property were by definition evil; and that the rich man was the prisoner of sin. Early in the second century, accepted apostolic teaching forbade Christians to live like those who did not earn their sustenance `by their own toil and sweat, but live by the unrighteous exploitation of other men's labour'.[2] Their refusal to worship the emperors or to carry arms appealed strongly to the oppressed and insecure. A generation later, a Christian leader in Rome, where rich converts were most numerous, pleaded that the rich man, though admittedly evil and unprofitable, might be of some service to the virtuous Christian poor, just as the barren elm supported the fruiting vine.

In 312, Christianity became a force to be reckoned with when the Roman Emperor, Constantine, was converted. In the following year, the Edict of Milan recognised Christianity as the Roman Empire's official religion, and Constantine set about uniting the Church to the secular state. His capital, Constantinople,[3] became the

---

1   Modern St Albans.
2   Quoted in Morris J. *Op cit:* p 12.
3   Formerly Byzantium, now Istanbul.

centre of the eastern Church but he left the bishop of Rome as the most prominent figure in the west. In Britain, organised Christianity was represented by bishoprics at York, London, and Colchester. The bishop of Colchester attended the Council of Arles in 314,[4] and there were three bishops from Britain at the Council of Rimini in 359.[5]

The leaders of western reform in the generation following Constantine's death in 377 were three outstanding contemporaries, Damasus, Ambrose of Milan, and Martin of Tours. Damasus became bishop of Rome in 366, taking the title *Pontifex Maximus*.[6] The title and the magisterial authority it conveyed made him the first bishop of Rome to whom the term `Pope' may be applied. Damasus cut a deliberately ostentatious figure:

> `... Riding in a carriage, wearing conspicuous clothes, keeping a table better than the emperor's.'[7]

Damasus gave Latin Christianity a powerful, visible, and efficient presence, and demonstrated the strength of its followers. He commissioned the scholar, Jerome, to prepare a single authoritative translation of the scriptures. Jerome's Latin text, the Vulgate, remains the canonical bible of the Latin Church.

Ambrose, bishop of Milan, combined the authority of the prelate with the humility of the priest. In 373, he was governor of north-eastern Italy when a hotly contested episcopal election threatened riots in Milan, and Ambrose was allegedly voted in by the crowd. Baptised, ordained, and consecrated within a week, he set out to adapt the eastern phenomenon of the monk to the urban Latin Church by encouraging ordained monks to live amongst men in order to set a visible example of a more

---

4   Frend W H C. The Christianisation of Roman Britain. In Barley M W, Hanson R P C. *Op cit.*

5   Myres J N L. Introducton. In *ibid:* p 4.

6   This was the title of the ancient chief priesthood of the City of Rome, a title held by Julius Caesar and all the emperors after him. Morris J. *Op cit:* p 23.

7   Ammianus Marcellinus, a historian who was also a serving officer in the Roman army. He wrote in the mid-fourth century. Quoted in Morris J. *Op cit:* p 24.

perfect life within ordinary society. In the following generation, many bishops induced all or part of their clergy to accept monastic vows, and the cathedral monastery became a symbol of reform. Ambrose's teaching was instrumental in the conversion to Christianity of Augustine of Hippo whose theology was to dominate the western Christian tradition. Augustine's doctrine of predestination made man's salvation entirely dependent on God's gift of grace, expressed through the Church and the sacraments, rather than the individual's free choice between good and evil.

Martin of Tours was a soldier who won a discharge from the Roman army as a conscientious objector. He settled as a hermit near Poitiers but was invited to Tours in 372, and in similar fashion to Ambrose, was acclaimed bishop by a large crowd of voters. Resuming his hermit's life in a cave outside Tours, Martin pioneered rural preaching and gathered around him a monastic cathedral school of some eighty pupils. Amongst these were Amator who became bishop of Auxerre and ordained the British monk, Patrick; and Vitricius, later bishop of Rouen who, in 396, carried Martin's teaching to Britain. Vitricius was a champion of the weak against oppression and wrote that:

`... Men do not differ by nature, but only in time and place, in their occupation and ideas, for difference is foreign to divine unity.'[8]

For his egalitarian views, Vitricius was warned by Pope Innocent that Rome condemned innovators whose presumption violated the purity of the Church by seeking the favour of the people rather than by fearing the judgement of God. Vitricius was the organiser of monks who renounced secular society as well as the pioneer of the extension of Christianity from townsmen and gentlemen to peasants and barbarians. The teaching of Vitricius had an immediate impact in Britain where, in 398, Ninian[9] dedicated a church to Martin in Whithorn, Galloway, from where he converted the southern Picts.

---

8   Quoted in *ibid:* p 336.
9   Bede says that Ninian was a British bishop trained in Rome. Bede. *Ecclesiastical History:* iii.4.

It was at this time that British ideas first made an impact on Mediterranean Christian thought. In Rome, the British monk, Pelagius, an esteemed theological writer, defended the humanist values which Christianity inherited from its Roman past. He denied the doctrine of original sin and maintained that the human will was capable of good without the help of divine grace. Man could contribute significantly to his own salvation by leading a moral life whose merit would claim recognition at the Day of Judgement.[10] This philosophy was a direct challenge to that of Augustine of Hippo, and when Rome fell to the Goths in 410, the followers of Pelagius were accused or usurping 'the authority of the catholic law'. All the known leaders of the most radical of the Pelagians were British, and their foremost exponent, known as the Sicilian Briton,[11] was the same individual who had expressed the hope that Rome's ruin would result in a 'holier' society. The Sicilian Briton's pamphlets all have a common opening statement:

'If thou wouldst be perfect, go sell all that thou hast.'[12]

This ideology was not new but he added a further thesis:

'Mankind is divided into three classes, the rich, the poor, and those who have enough ... abolish the rich and you will have no more poor ... for it is the few rich who are the cause of the many poor.'[13]

This was a unique concept in a society where Christian tradition went no further than simple denunciation of wealth and property as evil and un-Christian. Augustine seized his work, *On Riches*, and ordered his arrest. Pelagianism became heresy and was banned in 418.

At a time when the civilised world was being turned upside down, and anarchy was

---

10   Myres J N L. Introduction. In Barley M W, Hanson R P C. *Op cit.*
11   The Sicilian Briton's real name is unknown but he was obviously from a patrician family because he wrote home to a relative who was almost certainly a consul. Morris J. *Op cit:* p 48ff.
12   Quoted in *ibid:* p 340.
13   Quoted in *ibid:* p 341.

a very real threat, the theology of Augustine represented stability. It made man's salvation dependent on sacraments administered by a duly ordained priest in a disciplined hierarchy of bishops, metropolitans, and popes, which might preserve the unity of the Church in the event of dissolution of political authority. It must be remembered, too, that there was still a powerful pagan aristocracy in Rome which believed that Christian doctrine threatened the rights of property. It was Augustine (and also Damasus) who attempted to dispel these doubts in order to present Christianity as a faith for all humanity.[14] The ideologies which clashed were the most fundamental in Christian thinking; whether a man might commune directly with his god or whether he must depend upon the intermediary of a priest.[15]

Some ten years after the banning of the Pelagian heresy, it was revived in Britain by a bishop named Agricola. The Pope and the bishops of Gaul responded immediately by sending Germanus, the reforming bishop of Auxerre, to Britain.[16] In 429, Germanus was greeted in an official capacity at Verulamium by a gathering of wealthy landowners, luxuriously attired and accompanied by their supported tenantry.[17] Nevertheless, he found an active hostility of the poor against the rich which he turned to his advantage by preaching openly in the streets and countryside as well as in the churches. Like Ambrose of Milan, Germanus had once been a Roman officer so he was a good tactition and eminently capable of interpreting the mood of the people. When a group of Pelagians challenged him to a public debate, he made them look foolish by exposing their ostentatious dress and pretentious oratory.

Nevertheless, Germanus failed to win ecclesiastical support in Britain, and in 431, Pope Celestine appointed his own deacon, Palladius, as 'bishop to the Irish Christians'. Since most of the Irish were, as yet, unconverted, the appointment of one of the most eminent ecclesiastics in Europe to a barbarian outpost was, indeed, remarkable. Palladius was not well received, and tradition has it that he died within a year, on his

---

14 Morris J R. The literary evidence. In Barley M W, Hanson R P C. *Op cit.*

15 Modern theologians have remarked that Pelagius' philosophy has much in common with the later Protestantism of northern Europe. Morris J. *Op cit:* p 342.

16 Germanus was Amator's successor at Auxerre.

17 Myres J N L. *The English Settlements. Op cit:* p 205. Germanus also visited the tomb of St Alban in which he placed relics of all the apostles and martyrs claiming that all the saints were of equal merit in heaven.

way back to Rome. In his stead came Patrick, the son of a British landowner. Patrick had been captured into slavery by Irish raiders at the age of sixteen and trained in Gaul by the successors of Martin of Tours. He came from a Christian family; both his father and his grandfather had taken holy orders.[18] Patrick was a missionary first and a theologian second. He was the earliest British saint,[19] and the first regular bishop appointed by Rome to Ireland.

Patrick landed in Ireland in 432 and was received without enthusiasm by the High King Loegaire who, nevertheless, gave him licence to preach. Patrick's mission was partly motivated by the political situation of the time. The Irish had long been a thorn in the side of the British because of their frequent invasions into north and south Wales, Cornwall, and northern Britain. The British leader, Vortigern, in an attempt to subdue the Irish colonists in Britain, exacted a formal treaty with Loegaire which included marriage of his daughter to the High King's son. It was in Vortigern's interest that Loegaire's subjects embrace the religion of Britain, and certainly, following the dynastic marriage and Patrick's arrival, the ancient threat from Ireland ended as abruptly as that from the Picts.

Irish Christianity was a major influence in the formation of a new society in Britain. From the beginning of the fifth century, the people of Ireland submitted to the authority of a large number of petty local princes whose trivial and bloody feuds were to impoverish their subjects for centuries, and to dispose them to welcome the security of Christian monastic life. It was in the turmoil of a rapidly changing society and in a country without towns, that Irish Christianity was moulded. The acceptance of the new religion also joined Ireland to Britain. From the beginning of the sixth century, the history of the people of the British Isles are inseparable. They hang closely together because they were jointly exploring a new dimension in European civilisation. The mass conversion to Christianity in this century was the achievement of the monastic reformers. The new monasteries were the first form of Christianity that the bulk of the population encountered at close quarters.

---

18 Bieler L. St Patrick and the British Church. In Barley M W, Hanson R P C. *Op cit:* p 123.
19 Patrick is the only British saint whose own writings survive in *Confessio; Epistula ad Coroticum 357-380.* Cited in Morris J. *Op cit:* 347.

The most forceful among the younger monks who survived the devastating bubonic plague of the mid sixth century was Columba. He was a royal prince[20] whose enigmatic personality made as deep an impression on the history of mankind as any man of his century in Europe.[21] Columba established his first major monastery on his own family land at Derry but is also credited with the founding of a further twenty to forty houses which gave him enormous power and following. In 561, Columba raised an army against his dynastic rival, King Diarmait, over conflicts between the independence of the Church and the authority of the King's law. In the ensuing battle, Columba lost one man whilst Diarmait's losses amounted to three thousand. Given the political situation in Ireland where wars were fought in defence of individual dynastic territories, the military victory of an all-powerful royal abbot brought with it the threat of a divine monarch. A synod, therefore, condemned Columba's action, and accepting voluntary exile, he left Ireland for Iona where he remained to spread Christianity amongst the Picts. A monk from Columba's monastery on Iona moulded the church of Northumbria, and his later heirs were to win the greater part of England to Christianity and monasticism. Irish became the first medieval language to be written, and its monks became the intellectual inspiration of Europe.

In Britain, at this time, monks were few and monastic retreats were comfortable places, founded by gentry to escape the vicissitudes of secular life. Christianity was still the religion of royalty, noblemen, and townsmen; the language of the Church equated the country folk, *pagani*, with non-Christians. Almost nothing is known of the Church which Gildas denounced in about 540 when he complained of the excesses of the priests and bishops who condoned and shared the sins of the rulers and people. Gildas, himself, was trained at the monastic school in Llantwit, Glamorgan, founded by Iltud, one of the great teachers of the age.[22] This school was typical of those which boys entered at the age of about five and stayed a dozen years or more. Ordained monks such as Gildas, Samson, and Paul Aurelian were the influential monastic reformers of the age, adopting an austere piety with which the rural

---

20 Two of Columba's first cousins became High Kings of Ireland.
21 Morris J. *Op cit*: p 169.
22 Iltud was said to be Armorican and to have visited the court of King Arthur. Morris J. *Op cit*: p 121, 369.

population could identify and weave into their daily lives. There were ascetics in small numbers elsewhere in Europe but they became a mighty movement only in western Britain. Gildas praised the priests who had taken the monastic vow, and his writings gave cohesion to the new monasticism.[23] Many kings and wealthy men gave them land and welcomed and protected them. Some even gave up their estates to the monks and joined them as lay brothers. An estate placed under the control or protection of the monks ceased to be taxable and each new recruit to the monastery was one less labourer, taxpayer, or army recruit. Landlords and rulers had good reason to resent the monastic fervour but feared to condemn it.

The strength of the British monks was largely confined to Dumnonia, Brittany, and south Wales. In Wales, the most forceful of the monastic reformers was David who followed the rule of the stricter monks, refusing to accept land or endowments from laymen, and living a rigidly disciplined life of vigorous manual labour and prayer. Gildas accused David and his followers of arrogance and false pride. In his own monastery, the monks lived well upon the labours of their peasants.

British priests and monks made no attempt to convert the Saxon invaders who began to settle their lands and dispossess their kinsmen. The wandering Irish monks went to northern Britain or the Continent to satisfy their missionary zeal and did not set foot onto Saxon lands before the coming of Augustine. The strength of heathenism in the Saxon territories of central and south-east Britain should not be underestimated. More than nine-tenths of all the pagan place-names throughout the land were distributed within these areas of Saxon settlement.[24] Augustine and his missionaries can perhaps be forgiven for harbouring anxieties regarding their reception in the chilly climes of Britain because heathenism was still a living religion when it met the Christian challenge.

---

23 In old age, Gildas was summoned to Ireland following the departure of Columba to Iona to advise upon the future of the church in Ireland. Morris J. *Op cit:* p 174. Irish tradition acknowledged Gildas as its inspiration. Morris J R. The literary evidence. In Barley M W, Hanson R P C. *Op cit.*

24 Stenton, Sir F. *Op cit:* p 102.

Chapter 4
St Augustine's Mission

`Then he said to his disciples, `The harvest is rich but the labourers are few,
so ask the Lord of the harvest to send out labourers to his harvest.'

St Matthew 9: 37, 38

King Aethelberht of Kent was baptised at Pentecost in the year 597, within three
months of Augustine's arrival in Britain.[1] Towards the end of the year, Augustine sent
two members of the mission, Laurentius the priest and Peter the monk, to Rome with
an account of what had been achieved and a request for instruction on certain practical issues which he considered certain to arise in the future. The following summer,
Pope Gregory wrote to the patriarch of Alexandria with the news that over ten thousand Saxon converts had been baptised the previous Christmas Day in the River
Swale.[2] Gregory did not reply to Augustine's letter until the summer of 601[3] when
Laurentius and Peter returned to Britain as leaders of a second mission which included later bishops, Justus, Mellitus, and Paulinus. With the returning party, the Pope
sent a pallium for Augustine, vestments, plate, altar coverings, relics,[4] books, and two
copies of the Gospels.[5] There were also gifts and letters for Aethelberht and Bertha
whom Gregory chided for her delay in leading her husband to the Christian faith.[6]
They had, after all, been married for forty years.

---

1   The date of Aethelberht's baptism is disputed.
2   This must have been an exaggeration since the entire population of Kent cannot have been far short of this
    figure. Witney K P. *Op cit:* p 115. It is interesting to note that 25 December was the first day of the pagan
    New Year and was, therefore, an important festival for both heathen and Christian.
3   For Augustine's nine questions to the Pope and the latter's replies, see Bede. *Ecclesiastical History:* i.27. They
    were concerned with the conduct of Christians and the role of the Church and its clergy in society and in
    their own monastic communities.
4   The relics were said to include a part of the True Cross, hair of the Mother of God, a part of the rod of Jesse,
    and a piece of the Unsewn Tunic of Christ. Phillips, Father Andrew. *Op cit:* p 14.
5   Modern archbishops of Canterbury have taken their oaths on one of these Gospels which is held at Corpus
    Christi College, Cambridge.
6   *Councils and Ecclesiastical Documents.* Cited in Witney K P. *Op cit:* p 114

The figure of St Luke from the copy of the Gospels sent to Augustine by Pope Gregory. The book is written in a sixth-century Italian hand. (Reproduced with kind permission of the Master and Fellows of Corpus Christi College, Cambridge, MS 286, f. 129v).

Augustine had obviously felt uneasy about consecrating a bishop without the presence of other bishops but Gregory reminded him that he was, after all, the only representative of the Roman Church in Britain since the bishops of Gaul rarely visited. He was advised to continue consecrating bishops until he had enough to call on. The Pope's scheme for the future constitution of the Saxon Church included the beginnings of a marriage law as well as guidance for the services of baptism and mass. One of the questions which Augustine asked of Gregory was what to do about the divergences between the liturgical practices of Rome and Gaul. Should a Church which professed one faith be using different customs? Augustine would have become familiar with Gallican liturgy on his journey through Gaul and it is likely that this was also used by Bertha's chaplain in St Martin's Church. Gregory suggested, rather impatiently, that since the Church at Canterbury was untrammelled by tradition, Augustine should exploit the opportunity to gather the most pleasing features from the various churches and create the best possible liturgy for his new Church.[7] Augustine, however, did not heed this advice perhaps because, being of a conservative and disciplined nature, he could not bring himself to deviate from a rite which he had observed all his life. It is likely, too, that he had already established a theological presence in Canterbury which he was loathe to disrupt. It is important to remember that it was three and half years before Augustine received Pope Gregory's replies to his questions, during which time the archbishop had had the freedom, and had probably developed the confidence to break away from his mentor's influence.

Nevertheless, it is difficult to be certain of the exact rite used by Augustine and his followers although the Gelasian sacramentary would have been used in preference to the old Leonine or new Gregorian[8] sacramentaries since the first was a presbyteral and the others pontifical sacramentaries. Also, the structure of the `canon of the mass' as found in the ordines Romani was already fixed when Augustine arrived

---

7   Bede. *Ecclesiastical History*: i.27.
8   Gregory had revised the Gelasian sacramentary and brought the Eucharist to what he considered an elaborate perfection yet, as can be seen from his letter to Augustine, he was far from being a pedant on such points. Bright W. *Chapters of early English Church History*. Clarendon Press, Oxford 1888: p 59.

in Kent although a traditional freedom of phrasing was allowed to the celebrating bishop.[9] Augustine would have used the Gelasian canon of the mass which is substantially that found in the Roman missal of today. The Gallican rites known to Augustine were sister rites of those used by the Celtic Church.

It is possible to reconstruct a Eucharist service such as Augustine and his missionaries might have celebrated in one of the small, wooden churches at Canterbury. The mass began with the Offertory or Preparation with the congregation offering bread and perhaps wine or oil which was collected in a basket by the priest. When the clergy were robed in their long, white linen dalmatics they would enter from one of the porticus used as a sacristy. The presiding bishop wore a dark green chasuble and the pallium. A psalm was sung followed by prayers and readings. After these came an Entry Psalm (the Introit) with an antiphon sung after each verse. The deacon then intoned the litany to the chanting of *Kyrie eleison*, Lord have mercy.[10] Whether Augustine, as archbishop, would have sung the *Gloria in Excelsis*, introduced into the Gregorian by Pope Gregory, is uncertain. His priests would not. Collects were followed by the Epistle for the day, read by the clergy which had processed from the altar towards the congregation. The people bowed to the Gospel as Christ in person, and the clergy, carrying candles and incense, sang the gradual psalm as they walked to the pulpit in the nave where the Gospel was read in Latin,[11] followed possibly by an interpretation in the vernacular. The Eucharist prayer and consecration was followed by communion which was received by children and adults alike. The congregation stood throughout the service (seating in church was not introduced until the late Middle Ages).[12]

---

9   Deansly M. *The pre-conquest Church in England: an ecclesiastical history of England.* Adam & Charles Black, London 1963: p 154.

10   The *kyrie eleison* had been introduced by Pope Gregory for use on weekdays when he celebrated at the stational churches. *Ibid:* p 146.

11   There is no evidence that the Gospel was read in the vernacular in the sixth or seventh centuries either by the Celts or the Canterbury Christians. *Ibid:* p 147.

12   Phillips, Father Andrew. *Op cit:* p 13.

Sometime in the summer of 602 or 603, Augustine consecrated an old Roman church as his Canterbury see, naming it Christchurch. King Aethelberht gave the surrounding land and buildings to the Church. Pope Gregory had suggested that the old churches and pagan temples should not be destroyed but should be cleansed and consecrated for Christian worship because the people might be more willing to attend services if they were solemnised in places which they had formerly frequented. Since the people were also accustomed to holding sacrificial feasts, let them instead, on saints' festival days, build 'tabernacles' with boughs of trees and kill oxen for their meal with thanks to God, the Giver of all things.[13]

Augustine's missionaries led a communal but not a strictly monastic life, supported as a community by the revenues at their disposal. They would recite the *opus dei* and follow the Benedictine rule, but how far the rule of enclosure could be followed is not known. However, there was pastoral work to be done and it is likely that the community included youths and even children preparing for admission to holy orders since the first duty of any bishop at the time would have been the long training of a native clergy.[14] As these young candidates approached a suitable age, they were usually offered the option of marriage. The married clerk of or below the grade of *lector* (reader) had an important place in the organisation of a sixth century cathedral church.[15] A feature of early Saxon Christianity was almsgiving. Society as a whole was poor and there was no organisation for social relief. It was accepted that a third of the offerings made by the faithful at mass should go to the poor, and a large part of such a third would be used in the maintenance of a *hospitium* where strangers and pilgrims could be received and food distributed to the poor. It is likely that some such hostel was maintained from the earliest times at Canterbury for it was in accordance with canonical practice.[16]

13   Bede. *Ecclesiastical History:* i.30.
14   Stenton, Sir F. *Op cit:* p 108.
15   *Ibid:* p 108.
16   Deansley, M. *Op cit:* p 343.

To fulfil its mission the Church needed both royal protection and an ordered framework of society. In order to construct this, the king required instruments of literacy which only the Church or those trained in its schools could supply. The first use to which Aethelberht put the gift of literacy was in codifying the customs of the Kentish people. Aethelberht's laws are the oldest documents written in the English language and were formulated at the beginning of the seventh century. Augustine would almost certainly have encouraged and approved of this work and it was undoubtedly written by Christian scribes. It is to Augustine's credit that he made little attempt to influence the content of these first laws which, apart from one clause dealing with theft of church property, deal with the obligations of honour and blood-price typical of a pagan society where the feud was an accepted institution.[17] He was, no doubt, satisfied that, for the first time, these traditions were being encoded into a body of law.

The Pope directed Augustine to consecrate twelve bishops in the southern half of the country who would remain subject to him. He was also asked to send a bishop to York who would consecrate a further twelve bishops and act as their metropolitan although overall authority was to remain with Augustine.[18] In addition, Gregory intimated that Augustine should remove his seat from Canterbury to London at the earliest suitable opportunity. After Augustine's death, the see of York was to become independent of his successors and each successive metropolitan of York and London would receive the pallium from the Pope. Their precedence would be determined by seniority of consecration. This division of England into two equal ecclesiastical provinces reflected the politics of the age with Northumbria being ruled by King Aethelfirth and all the land south of the Humber and east of the Severn coming under the rule of Aethelberht.

---

17   Witney K P. *Op cit:* p 93.
18   The figure of twenty-four dioceses was reached only under Henry VIII who was then to undo the Church. Phillips, Father Andrew. *Op cit:* p 15.

In 604, a second Kentish see was established in a church dedicated to St Andrew and built by Aethelberht at Rochester which had been an important Roman town. Justus, a member of the second mission, was appointed bishop. In this year too, Aethelberht built a church in honour of St Paul on the highest ground within the City of London, and Mellitus was consecrated bishop. This was a bold move since London was the chief town of the East Saxons and beyond the sphere of Aethelberht's direct rule. Nevertheless, his sister's son, Saberht, was king of Essex, and Aethelberht must have felt confident that he would not be thwarted. Saberht, himself, had been converted to Christianity. In these early days, episcopal sees were established in the old Roman cities which had been allowed to decay for almost two hundred years since the collapse of the Empire. Despite being served by men who had once lived as monks, none of these early cathedrals were monasteries. The only English monastery known to have been founded in Augustine's time was that of St Peter and St Paul just outside the east wall of Canterbury where Peter became abbot and Augustine, who did not live to consecrate its church, was buried.

King Aethelberht's gifts to the monastery included a large silver paten, a gold sceptre, and a golden bit and saddle adorned with gems.[19] Later, in 978, the Church of St Peter and St Paul was enlarged and reconstructed by Dunstan, archbishop of Canterbury, and from this time the monastery was known as St Augustine's Abbey.

Gregory placed the British bishops of the Celtic Church under Augustine's authority:

`... that the unlearned may be instructed, the weak strengthened by your counsel, and the perverse corrected by your authority.'[20]

19   Thorne. Cited in *ibid:* p 117.
20   Bede. *Ecclesiastical History:* i.27.

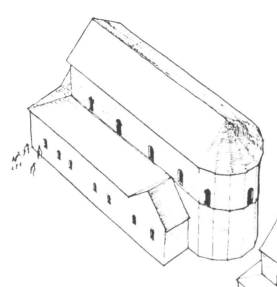

The church built on the site of St Augustine's monastery of St Peter and St Paul, Canterbury. (Drawing by Terry Ball from a reconstruction by Richard Gem in Sparks M, *St Augustine's Abbey*. English Heritage, London 1996. Reproduced with kind permission of English Heritage).

The remains of St Augustine's Abbey founded in 598 and rebuilt after the Norman conquest. The photograph shows some of the early Saxon foundations, the north wall of the nave (c 1090), and the base of the King Aethelberht Tower (demolished in 1822). In the background is the central tower of Canterbury Cathedral. (Photograph by the author)

The bishops of Gaul, however, were to remain independent since Gregory's predecessors had granted the pallium to the bishop of Arles, and their precedent must be followed. In a separate letter to the bishop of Arles, Gregory was careful to define Augustine's position. Augustine, himself, took a less autocratic approach to the Celtic Church. Unlike the Pope, he had hands on experience of the situation. On two occasions he met with British bishops and church leaders in an attempt to secure their co-operation with his mission. His aim was to secure conformity with Roman practice regarding baptism ritual and the computation of Easter,[21] as well as persuading them to join him in the conversion of the Saxons. He was, however, prepared to compromise on lesser differences.

The first meeting with British church leaders was held in 603 at a place later called St Augustine's Oak, variously identified at Aust, Malmesbury and other locations in Worcestershire or the Cotswolds. There was, apparently, much fruitless disputation which culminated in a trial of spiritual strength between the two sides as to who could restore the sight of a blind Saxon. Augustine won the contest[22] and the British agreed to a second meeting, the venue for which was probably the border town of Abberley, Worcestershire. It was here that tradition preserved the name of an ancient tree called Apostle's Oak. Seven British bishops and a number of learned monks from the monastery of Bangor-is-Coed met Augustine and his retinue. The second meeting is said to have failed because Augustine remained seated when approached by the British ecclesiastics, thus demonstrating his superiority over them rather than present himself on equal terms with them as a humble servant of Christ. There were undoubtedly other reasons for a breach between the Roman mission and the British churches, not least of which was the latter's uncompromising

---

21 In 455, Pope Leo introduced a method of calculating Easter which the British and Irish had failed to adopt. This resulted in a discrepancy of as much as thirty days between the dates on which they and the Roman Church celebrated the feast. Witney K P. *Op cit:* p 120. The British took the vernal equinox to be the 25th rather than the 21st March.

22 Pope Gregory, in a letter to Augustine dated 1 June 601, had exhorted him not to incur the danger of becoming elated by the success of his miracles. 'For not all the elect work miracles, but nevertheless all their names are written in heaven.' Bede. *Ecclesiastical History:* i.31.

antipathy to the salvation of the Saxons whom they despised. Superficially, at least, the ascetic monastic tradition of the British had little in common with the humane Italian monasticism in which Augustine and his companions had been trained. If the British ecclesiastics accepted Roman supremacy there was a risk of losing not only their religious identity but of undermining the political independence of their territory. Subordination to Augustine meant subordination to his patron, King Aethelberht who, as Bretwalda of southern Britain and the most powerful royal representative of Roman Christendom in the land, might be encouraged to attempt unification of the English states under one sovereign.[23]

The rebuff of the British bishops to Augustine's approach marked a watershed in the progress of the Roman mission and in Kentish hegemony. Augustine's mission had always been fraught with difficulties. He attempted the conversion of a people whose culture was alien, and he was confronted with the hostile clergy of an ancient church. No doubt there were many among the Kentish peoples who believed that it was possible to accept a new god and to please the king by doing so, without abandoning all belief in the old ones. Indeed, conversion to Christianity did not mean that the convert ceased to be a pagan. For centuries, people who attended mass on Sunday mornings, sacrificed to their household gods on Sunday afternoon.[24] Between 670 and 690, Archbishop Theodore found it necessary to appoint penances for those 'Christians' who sacrificed to devils, foretold the future with their aid, ate food which had been offered in sacrifice, or burned barley in a house where there had been a death to ensure protection of the living.[25,26]

23   Aethelberht's main rival, Aethelfirth of Northumbria, was a pagan.
24   Morris J. *Op cit:* p 27.
25   Stenton, Sir F. *Op cit:* 128.
26   Witney K P. *Op cit:* 112.

Pope Gregory passed away in 605, and Augustine on 26 May in an unknown year between 604 and 609. The epitaph inscribed on Augustine's tomb read:

`Here lies the most reverend Augustine, first archbishop of Canterbury, who was formerly sent hither by St Gregory, bishop of Rome; being supported by God in the working of miracles, he led King Aethelberht and his nation from the worship of idols to faith in Christ and ended the days of his office in peace.'[27]

It was Aethelberht's misfortune to survive for a further decade, declining impotently into old age, a king in name only and already superseded in the *Bretwaldship* by his younger contemporary, Raedwald of the East Angles who was a warrior king in the old tradition.

The site of St Augustine's first grave in a north porticus of the church of St Peter and St Paul. In this small chamber, the first Archbishop of Canterbury was buried with five of his successors. Their relics were removed to new shrines in 1091. (Photograph by the author)

27 Bede. *Ecclesiastical History*: ii.4.

It has been said that Augustine was not himself a great man but that he had greatness thrust upon him.[28] He was a legalist rather than an evangelist; a priest rather than a prophet. He was a man of narrow views, tending to the unimaginative, uncomfortable with the unfamiliar. Nevertheless, he was without doubt a devout and tireless Christian missionary, persevering in the face of what, at times, must have been an onerous and difficult task. His apostolate in England was short, probably little more than seven years, but he restored the connection with Rome and brought the Saxons into the orbit of ecclesiastical civilisation. He did his duty as it had been entrusted to him by Pope Gregory and his achievement would never be undone.

Shortly before he died, Augustine consecrated Laurentius his successor,[29] and the priority of the new archbishop was to re-establish relations with the Celtic Church. In association with bishops Mellitus of London and Justus of Rochester, he wrote to the bishops and abbots of the Irish Church exhorting them to accept the Roman computation of Easter. The contact was obviously unfriendly since an Irish bishop named Dagan refused to join them in either food or lodging. A similar attitude prevailed amongst the Welsh. Well into the seventh century, the clergy in Dyfed would not associate with the English in church, nor eat from the same dishes. They even threw the remnants of a shared meal to the dogs and scoured the dishes as being contaminated.[30]

Communication between Rome and Canterbury was maintained although the missionaries must have been loathe, at times, to report their lack of progress in the general acceptance of Christianity. Mellitus attended a Roman synod held by Pope Boniface IV on 27 February 610 and returned with letters from the Pope Boniface IV

28 Godfrey J. *Op cit:* p 90.
29 Stenton, Sir F. *Op cit:* p 112. As Laurentius never received the pallium it is likely that his position was regarded as uncanonical in Rome.
30 *Adhelmi Opera.* Ed Ehwald R (MGH): p 484. Cited in *ibid:* 103. Letter from Adhelm to Geraint, King of Dumnonia.

to Laurentius and Aethelberht. King Raedwald of East Anglia was induced by Aethelberht to accept baptism but none of his subjects followed him, and Raedwald himself was buried in the full splendour of a pagan king. If the magnificence of his burial goods at Sutton Hoo were typical of the royal treasure chests of the day, then it is easy to imagine the style in which the richest and most powerful rulers of the Dark Ages lived.[31] Amongst Raedwald's possessions were a pair of silver spoons engraved in Greek characters with the names of Saul and Paul. It is possible that these were baptism gifts from King Aethelberht himself.[32]

At Aethelberht's death in 616, the Kentish court was not yet wholly Christian. Eadbald, his son and successor, had never been baptised and in the pagan Germanic tradition, he immediately married his father's widow.[33] Whatever his beliefs, Eadbald was not cast in the same mould as his father, and the kings of southern Britain rejected allegiance to both him and to Christianity. Upon the death of Aethelberht's nephew, King Saberht of the East Saxons, his three pagan sons drove bishop Mellitus from London because he refused to give them the eucharist bread which he had given to their father. Both Mellitus and Justus of Rochester fled to Gaul. Tradition has it that Laurentius would have followed but for a visitation from St Peter who chastised and scourged him severely. Eadbald was so unnerved by the marks of the scourge that he was converted to Christianity. Justus was then able to return to Rochester but it was a further forty years before another bishop could be consecrated for the East Saxons. Laurentius died in about 619 and was succeeded by Mellitus who lived until 624. Thereafter, Justus was transferred from Rochester to Canterbury, and upon his death in 627, the succession passed to Honorius, a member of one of the original missions, who was archbishop until 652.

---

31   The Sutton Hoo burial ship and treasures were discovered in 1939 and are now in the British Museum.

32   Witney K P. *Op cit:* p 104.

33   Eadbald married his stepmother. The date of Bertha's death is unknown. Pope Gregory, in his letter to Augustine dated 601, recognised this tradition amongst the Saxons but declared such unions unlawful once they were converted to Christianity. Bede. *Ecclesiastical History:* i.27.

Silver spoons found at Sutton Hoo and engraved with the names of Saul and Paul. They were probably baptism gifts to King Raedwald of East Anglia from King Aethelberht. (Courtesy of the Trustees of the British Museum, London, 1939.10-10.88-89)

In the meantime, Aethelfirth took advantage of the upheavals in the royal courts of the south and marched from Northumbria against Raedwald who was sheltering his rival, Edwin of Deira. Aethelfirth was defeated and Edwin took his place in the north. In 625, Edwin married Aethelberg, Christian daughter from Aethelberht's second marriage, and in the same year he assumed the *Bretwaldship* upon the death of Raedwald. Aethelberg had all the qualities which were lacking in her brother, and some idea of her personality may be gleaned from her nickname, Tata, which means 'merry'.[34] Edwin, himself a pagan, promised that his wife's religion would be respected and that he might even consider conversion. Accordingly, Paulinus, a member of the second mission of 601, was consecrated a bishop at Canterbury, and sent north with Aethelberg.

The story of Edwin's conversion, whilst not as dramatic as that of his brother-in-law, contains an element of the mystical. During his exile at Raedwald's East Anglian court, he had been visited by a stranger who had assured him of safety and a future kingdom in return for a promise of obedience when a man resembling the stranger should give an appointed sign. Edwin appears to have identified Paulinus with the stranger and to have accepted his conversion as repayment of a debt of honour. He was baptised at York on Easter Day, 627, in a wooden church dedicated to St Peter which he had built for the occasion.[35] A rapid extension of Christianity followed in the north until Edwin's death on 12 October 632 at Hatfield, near Doncaster, when Northumbria was beaten in battle by the upstart power of King Caedwallon of Gwynedd and his allies of Mercia.[36] In the aftermath, Paulinus fled to Kent with Aethelburg and her two small children, and was installed in the vacant bishopric at Rochester. Thereafter, for many years, Christianity in Northumbria owed more to the achievement of Celtic monks.

---

34   The name 'Aethelberg' means 'noble city'.
35   Edwin's church was on the site of the present York Minster. Bede. *Ecclesiastical History:* ii.14.
36   Mercia means 'boundary folk' and the territory occupied by its 12,000 households included all the country from the lower Trent to the forests of the west midlands. Tamworth was the chief residence of its kings. Stenton, Sir F. *Op cit:* p 40.

However, in East Anglia, the Christian king, Sigeberht, looked to Canterbury to help in establishing a church. Archbishop Honorius sent a Burgundian bishop named Felix, to establish a see at Dunwich, and the future of the East Anglian church was secured by the foundation of a school for which Felix obtained teachers from Kent. The importance attached to educational activities and the excellence of its scholars marks the real strength of the Kentish mission.

By the end of the seventh century, the church in Kent had become a major landowner. In addition to the monastery of St Peter and St Paul, and Christchurch in Canterbury, there were religious houses with considerable estates at Reculver, Minster in Thanet, Sheppey, Dover, Folkestone, and Lyminge. These all had their own tenants, labourers, craftsmen and workshops, producing surplus for both trade and barter for raw materials. Excavations of the churches which Augustine and his immediate successors built show that they were Italianate in design and construction, and the builders who worked on them were almost certainly from Italy. Canterbury remained the capital of the Roman Church in England although Pope Gregory had never envisaged it as such. An attempt by the Mercian king, Cenwulf, at the end of the eighth century, to move the archiepiscopal seat to London (which was then under his control) failed on the unwillingness of the Pope to break an attachment cherished by churchmen throughout England.

The remains of the monastic church at Reculver showing the Norman towers and the ruins of the Saxon building. Reculver was probably one of the landing places of the invading Roman army and was one of the earliest defence posts in the command of the Saxon shore. (Photograph by the author)

> ‡ Chapel converted into a Cottage.
> ‡‡ House demolished by the Sea in 1782
> ‡‡‡ Explosion of a Powder-Mill at Faversham.
> ‡‡‡‡ Isle of Sheppey.

The monastic church at Reculver, depicted in a late eighteenth century engraving. In 669, King Egbert of Kent gave this site to build a monastery. The monastery church was built in the centre of an old Roman fort with the monastic buildings to the north. In the tenth century, the Saxon monastery was given to the Archbishopric of Canterbury and the church was used by the local people as a parish church until the early nineteenth century. All the monastery buildings have since been eroded away by the sea. (Reproduced with kind permission of English Heritage)

Chapter 5
St Augustine's Legacy

`By the grace of God which was given to me, I laid the foundations like a trained master-builder, and someone else is building on them. Now each one must be careful how he does the building.'

I Corinthians 3: 10

Following his conversion to Christianity, King Eadbald of Kent married Emma, a Frankish princess, and maintained the contacts with the Continent established by his father. His support of the Church helped keep the faith alive during this period of weakness and isolation, and he was responsible for the endowment of considerable estates to the Church. On the death of his brother-in-law, Edwin of Northumbria, Eadbald sheltered his sister, Aethelburg, and her children in Kent. Aethelberg became abbess of a monastery at Lyminge which was founded and endowed for her. She was the first in a long line of Kentish noblewomen and princesses to adopt the religious life. Both Lyminge and Folkestone were, in the Frankish tradition, double houses,[1] containing men as well as women, although presided over by the abbess.

In the north, Christianity was restored by Celtic missionaries from Iona led by Bishop Aidan of Lindisfarne. Under Aidan's directive, the first communities of religious women began to appear in Northumbria. It was Aidan himself who persuaded Hild, the greatest of all British abbesses, to follow religion in her own country and not in Gaul. Hild was abbess of the monastery at Whitby where, in 633, King Oswiu

---

I   These monasteries offered entirely separate facilities for men and women.

summoned the synod to determine, once and for all, whether the Celtic or Roman computation of Easter should be followed. The situation had become impossible, dividing communities and even families. In the royal Northumbrian household, Oswiu adhered to the Celtic system while his wife, Eanfled, daughter of Edwin and Aethelberg, followed the Roman practice, as did their son, Alhfrith. It was a young priest of Ripon named Wilfred who swayed the council in favour of Rome by declaring allegiance to St Peter rather than St Columba since it was the former who had been granted the keys of heaven. Tradition has it that King Oswiu closed the debate with a smile, suggesting that his own resistance to the Roman Church was weak. This is probably not surprising given that he had been married to Aethelberht's granddaughter for nearly twenty years and that Eanfled,[2] herself, had been instrumental in Wilfred's early training, sending him first to Kent and then to Lyons and Rome where he had studied for five years.

By the time of the Synod of Whitby, every Saxon kingdom except Sussex, contained the seat of a bishopric, and the five years following the synod were the most critical for the establishment of Christianity in the tradition of Augustine. King Earconberht, Eadbald's son and successor in Kent, was the first Saxon king to order not only the destruction of all pagan idols but also the observance of Lent. In addition, he forged Christian alliances with other kingdoms through dynastic marriages as well as establishing spiritual links with the Continent which later became important missionary routes. Long before paganism was dead in Britain, itself, individual missionaries were working in lands from which their ancestors had come to Britain. All of them were monks, and it was through the foundation of monasteries that Christianity was ultimately established in Frisia and in western and central Germany.

2   Aelfflaed, a daughter of Oswiu and Eanfled became abbess of Whitby after Hild's death in 680, ruling over it jointly with her mother. Bede. *Ecclesiastical History:* iv.26.

This Celtic cross was erected in 1884 by Granville George Levenson Gower, the second Earl of Granville and Lord Warden of the Cinque Ports, to commemorate the landing at Ebbsfleet of St Augustine in 597. (Photograph by the author)

St Augustine's cross was carved in Birmingham by J Roddis and is almost seven metres high. Its tapering shaft is covered with archbishops, angels, and beasts. (Photograph by the author)

Every ecclesiastical statesman of the seventh century regarded the monastic order as essential to the life of the Church. The founder of a monastery was free to determine the rule by which he and his companions would live. Christianity had been introduced into Saxon Britain by monks trained in the Benedictine tradition, and the church which owed its foundation to Gregory the Great was bound to revere the monastic saint whom Gregory regarded as his master. The adoption of St Benedict's rule in England is associated with Wilfred's circle but long before Wilfred's death, the Benedictine rule was observed in many houses with which he had never been connected.[3]

---

3   The rule of St Benedict was followed until the eleventh century when there was a sudden outburst of variations such as those followed by the Cluniac, Cistercian, and Savigniac houses.

On 26 March 668, the Pope Vitalian consecrated as archbishop of Canterbury, a sixty-six year old monk and scholar named Theodore who was a native of Tarsus, the city of Paul. Theodore was accompanied from Rome to Canterbury by Hadrian who became abbot of St Peter and St Paul's monastery, and by Benedict Biscop, a friend of Wilfred who was now bishop of Ripon. Within two years of his arrival, Theodore had appointed bishops to Lichfield, Rochester, Dunwich, and Winchester, and on 26 September 672, he summoned to Hertford the first general council of the whole English Church. The synod was an affirmation of the essential unity of the English Church under the authority of the archbishop.

During his rule, Theodore reorganised the English dioceses in order to make them more manageable. Each kingdom outside Kent constituted a single diocese, some of which (Northumbria, for example) were extremely large. Theodore doubled the existing sees from seven to fourteen, dividing Wilfred's powerful Northumbrian diocese into three. This had the effect of increasing the profile of the Church throughout the land since the bishops took an important role in every stage of the process by which the population was received into the Christian faith. Indeed, the state of religion in any part of England depended on the activity of its bishops. Only a minority of the clergy ever rose to the priesthood, and the division of a diocese into parishes, each under the spiritual charge of its own priest, was still a remote ideal at this time. The word *mynster* is Old English for the Latin *monasterium*, and many ancient parish churches represent early monasteries which disappeared without trace. The missionary impulse was strong in early English monasticism, and the foundation of a monastery was a natural means of spreading Christianity among a pagan people. Even at the end of the eighth century, many longstanding Christian communities were still unprovided with any form of church. Archbishop Theodore allowed priests to say mass `in the field', and the history of the standing cross dates from his time.

Theodore remained at Canterbury until his death on 19 September 690 and is remembered as a great ecclesiastical statesman under whose leadership the last of the pagan Saxon tribes accepted Christianity.[4] Theodore's disciples collected together the penances and ecclesiastical canons which he formulated for the internal order of the Church and for the regulation of Christian life. These laws came to influence the whole penitential system of the western world. In addition, the oldest English charters date from the time when Theodore was reorganising the English church.[5] By the end of the seventh century, a long series of such documents was evidence of the permanence which Theodore's rule had given to English ecclesiastical institutions.

The second Kentish law was issued in 695 by King Wihtred, grandson of Earconberht. In this document, the Church was declared free from taxation, the oath of a bishop, like the oath of a king, was declared incontrovertible, and the Church received the same compensation as the king for violence to dependents. King Ine of Wessex was the first ruler outside Kent to produce a code of custom based on a fusion of ancient tradition and new Christian values.[6] The Code of West Saxon Law, dated about 694, is the work of a responsible statesman determined to advance the cause of Christianity. Ine's laws were copied out by King Alfred as an appendix to the great code with which the continuity of English legislation begins. Ine is associated with the first West Saxon synods and he also founded the important see of Sherborne which was later moved to Salisbury.

---

4   The people of the Isle of Wight were the last to be converted. This was accomplished by Wilfred's sister's son, Beornwine.

5   The oldest charter is dated May 679. Stenton, Sir F. *Op cit:* p 141.

6   King Ine was associated with Wihtred of Kent.

Within a century and a half of the arrival of Augustine's mission, England had become the home of a Christian culture which influenced the whole development of letters and learning in western Europe. The origins of organised learning in England are rooted in the schools established by Augustine for the instruction of children who might proceed to holy orders, and continuous teaching was probably maintained at Canterbury throughout the seventh century. The school at Canterbury, particularly under Theodore, attracted scholars from distant centres of learning and provided an organised body of knowledge based on the interpretation of the scriptures as well as astronomy, music, poetry, Latin and Greek, and Roman law. It provided a classical education unrivalled by any other learned community north of the Alps and produced pupils such as Aldhelm of Malmesbury and Benedict Biscop who spent two years as abbot of Augustine's monastery of St Peter and St Paul before founding his own monastery (also called St Peter and St Paul) at Wearmonth and Jarrow in Northumbria.[7] It was Benedict Biscop who collected the finest library outside Italy[8] which made possible the work of the most important scholar of the age, the Venerable Bede.

7 These monasteries housed six hundred monks. Phillips, Father Andrew. *Op cit:* p 22.

8 Benedict Biscop made six visits to Rome, each time returning with a great treasure of books and relics. Deansley, M. *Op cit:* p 113

St Augustine of Canterbury, a detail from the Royal Window in the North West Transept, Canterbury Cathedral. This window was begun in 1482 and probably given by King Edward IV. Work was stopped when the King died in 1483, and completed by 1486. (Reproducedby kind permission of the Dean and Chapter of Canterbury Cathedral).

In his *Ecclesiastical History*, Bede recorded the words of Pope Gregory the Great who honoured the achievement of Augustine's mission:

'Lo, the mouth of Britain, which once only knew how to gnash its barbarous teeth, has long since learned to sing the praises of God with the alleluia of the Hebrews. See how the proud Ocean has become a servant, lying low now before the feet of the saints, and those barbarous motions, which earthly princes could not subdue with the sword, are now, through the fear of God, repressed with a simple word from the lips of priests; and he who, as an unbeliever, did not flinch before troops of warriors, now, as a believer, fears the words of the humble.'[9]

In 747, at the Synod of Clovesho, chaired by Archbishop Cuthbert of Canterbury, it was recommended that the feasts of St Gregory (12 March) and St Augustine of Canterbury (26 May) be celebrated throughout England as national festivals.[10] By the time of the Norman Conquest there were at least ten thousand churches and chapels in England for a population of one and a half millions. There were also thirty-five monasteries and nine convents housing some one thousand religious.[11] Within three months of the landing of William of Normandy at Pevensey on Michaelmas eve 1066, Anglo-Saxon England ceased to exist. William was crowned at Westminster Abbey on Christmas Day, and during the next four years he established his position as conqueror through a sustained destruction of the English way of life.[12] In the spring of 1070, William allowed all the monasteries in England to be plundered of their rich heritage of books, plate, embroideries, vestments, and relics.[13] He effectively drew a curtain between England and Rome, considering himself head of the Catholic Church in England and admitting papal legates only as envoys to the king, not as

9   Bede. *Ecclesiastical History:* ii.1.
10   Phillips, Father Andrew. *Op cit:* p 19.
11   *Ibid:* p 22.
12   Stenton, Sir F. *Op cit:* p 598ff.
13   Savage A (ed). *The Anglo-Saxon Chronicles. Op cit.* Entry for the year 1070.

plenipotentiaries with authority over the English Church.[14]   He replaced English abbots, priests, and even the archbishop of Canterbury[15] with Norman churchmen.

Many English ecclesiastics as well as substantial numbers of the population emigrated to the Continent in much the same way as the British had fled to Brittany following the invasion of the Saxons. In 1075, a fleet of three hundred and fifty ships left England for exile in the lands around the Black Sea, under the command of the Earl of Gloucester.   About four and a half thousand of these exiles settled in Constantinople and sent their priests to Hungary to be consecrated bishops since the English preferred the Latin rite to that of the Greek.[16]

One of the English exiles, tentatively identified as a holy man named Coleman, had been educated at St Augustine's Abbey. He built a basilica in the Byzantine City which he dedicated to St Nicholas and St Augustine of Canterbury.[17] Augustine's veneration in Constantinople by the descendents of the people whom he had brought to Christianity seems all the more remarkable in view of the fact that he had probably spent at least six years of his early life as a monk in the City with his friend and adviser, Gregory the Great. On the south side of the basilica was placed a painted icon of St Augustine and above it was written an inscription in Greek:

'St Augustine, Apostle of the English'

---

14   Godfrey J. *Op cit:* p 432.

15   William chose Archbishop Lanfranc, formerly abbot of Caen, to be primate over England. Lanfranc initiated the building of new cathedral churches at Canterbury, Lincoln, Salisbury, Rochester, Ely, and Winchester as well as many other Norman churches which are still intact. *Ibid:* p 411ff.

16   Phillips, Father Andrew. *Op cit:* 31.

17   The ruins of this basilica were said to be still visible in the nineteenth century at a place called Bogdan Sarai. *Ibid:* p 33.

Index